CW00404390

MANIC STREET PREACHERS
FROM DESPAIR TO WHERE

PHOTOGRAPHIC CREDITS

© ALL ACTION

© LONDON FEATURES INTERNATIONAL LTD.

© PICTORIAL PRESS

© POPPERFOTO

© REDFERNS

© REX PICTURES

© STEVE DOUBLE

UFO Music Ltd 18 Hanway Street London W1P 9DD England
Telephone: 0171 636 1281   Fax: 0171 636 0738

First published in Great Britain 1997
UFO Music Ltd 18 Hanway Street
London W1P 9DD

The author and publishers have made every effort to contact all copyright holders. Any who for any reason have not been contacted are invited to write to the publishers so that a full acknowledgment may be made in subsequent editions of this work.

ISBN 1-873884-79-6

Designed by UFO Music Ltd

MANIC STREET PREACHERS
FROM DESPAIR TO WHERE

BY JODY THOMPSON

CHAPTER 01
HERE AND 4 REAL

Norwich is, as the signs proudly proclaim, as you breach its outskirts, a fine city. A place famed for mustard, a stout-hearted football team and an exquisite Norman cathedral. Charming and picturesque, it is not a place naturally associated with rock legend. But it was here, on May 15 1991 that one of the most startling, disturbing and infamous events in British pop history took place, one that would take its place in rock mythology along with The Sex Pistols swearing on television, Kurt Cobain shooting himself or Jimi Hendrix burning his guitar. I know, I was there.

It happened at Norwich Arts Centre, an old converted church down a narrow alleyway off St Benedicts Street, one of Norwich city centre's many quaint and quirky ancient streets. Before, it had seen the likes of Nirvana and The Stone Roses, and was later to play host to Oasis. But that night, a band called the Manic Street Preachers were headlining and I was to interview them for the evening show I did on Livewire, the University Of East Anglia's radio station.

HERE AND 4 REAL

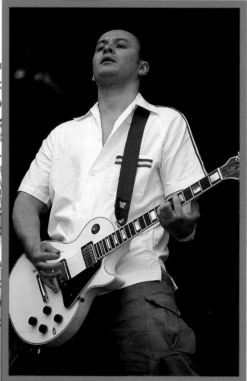

Despite the success in the indie charts of their single 'Motown Junk' in October 1990, some aspects of the music press and music buying public were wary of these sloganeering upstarts from Wales. They had noisily gatecrashed the alternately low-key, navel-pondering shoegazing or loutishly hedonistic baggy indie scene of the time, smeared with mascara and spouting political polemic. As a result, many people were intrigued but not convinced, which is much how I felt about them back then. Cartoon Clash? A recycled Ruts? A post-post modern PIL? It was time to make up my mind.

The interview was to take place at the end of the gig, so my friend Sandy and I, who I'd dragged along for the evening, got our drinks and joined the sparse crowd of about 40 in the gothic surrounds of the venue to watch the show.

Taking to the stage in their-then trademark T-shirts emblazoned with stencils of their latest buzzwords, the four piece didn't take long to capture the imagination of the initially apathetic audience. One by one, they stopped studying the engraved tombstones on the floor and raised their eyes to the stage where once the church altar had stood. And some, no doubt, were converted by the magic of the Manics there and then.

Looking like a Hanoi Rocks for the Nineties, they were punky and haphazard but seemed determined to the point of fury that they would get the attention of everyone present. As they pounded through their set, even though musically ragged round the edges, they seemed to be giving 100 per cent effort to prove that they were for real.

Nicky Wire on bass pouted shyly and did the rock star moves as Sean hid behind his drums. James sung with the kind of forceful passion that makes veins bulge on your neck in sympathy, with a voice since described as the finest white soul voice since Rod Stewart crossed with Bruce Springsteen, with a hint of Tina Turner, while Richey kept to the right side of the stage, eyes down, intent on his guitar playing.

A handful of female fans bedecked in leopard skin and glitter stood rapt at the foot of the stage from the beginning, but slowly a gaggle of more wary gig goers began to surround them down at the front, nodding their heads. When the band played their current single at that point 'You Love Us' the people politely pogoed. Nothing manic, but people were more impressed than they were sceptical. By the end of the rather short set, which was brimming with bravado, they had been mostly been won over. It was something of a result, especially considering Norwich audiences are traditionally hard to win over.

As the rabble wandered out of the dark building and into a darker night, we hung around waiting for the band to emerge from backstage. Nicky eventually appeared clutching a can and shyly proffered his hand when I introduced myself. He smiled sweetly and said the rest of the band would join us soon and the idea was that Steve Lamacq, the NME journalist, would do the first interview, but that I would join them and take my turn afterwards.

First Sean, then Richey, then James sauntered out from the depths of the old church and we walked through the detritus of fag ends and plastic beer glasses to the steps at the back of the hall which led up to the exit and the bar.

We sat down and the interview began. The chat was of the normal kind, about band influences, their agenda, what they wanted to achieve, what they stood for. But then Steve began

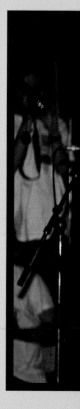

to question the band's authenticity, whether they were a patische of punk, mere faking actors of no substance, or the real thing. The band became visibly exasperated as the question had been raised regularly in the music press in the weeks preceding the interview.

Eventually, after a reasonably good mannered discussion lasting about half an hour, Steve and the band agreed to disagree.

What happened next is a bit of a blur. It is like trying to remember a film you watched long ago when hallucinating with a fever. The whole thing didn't seem real, seemed to happen in slow motion. Richey asked for a private word with Steve and the pair went backstage. What became apparent moments later was that while I was chatting to the others, Steve once again articulated to Richey the idea that the Manics were not for real. At this point, Richey produced a razor blade and calmly moved it up and down his thin forearm, slowly carving '4 REAL' into his white skin and said, "We're not the next Birdland, we do mean what we do."

As other members of the band and I were just warming up for our interview, Richey and Steve came back through. By the time we realised what had happened, Richey had wandered past us up the stairs to go to the toilets near the bar, followed by a shocked Lamacq.

When the reality of what had occurred sunk in - and it seemed to take an age - we went through to the foyer to see what was going on, in a somewhat fuzzy and unbelieving state.

An eerily tranquil Richey eventually came out of the toilet by which time we had summoned the Arts Centre staff and found a first aid kit. Sandy and I, numbed to the situation, managed to bandage his mutilated arm, which surreally reminded me at the time of an uncooked sausage roll, scored and ready for baking. The skin gaped where the razor had sliced exposing the blood and flesh beneath, deepest where he had started on the '4'. The image has haunted me ever since.

Just when we had finished wrapping the damaged limb, Ed Sirrs, the NME photographer appeared and said he wanted a photograph of the self-inflicted weals. I remember arguing with him that we'd just dressed the arm and it should stay that way. I couldn't believe he wanted the bandages removed once more, exposing the wounds to infection because he wanted a sensationalist snap of the handiwork of what was obviously a troubled mind. I angrily told him he was behaving no less badly or salaciously than a Fleet Street tabloid. But Richey had no qualms and looking back, I was being irrelevant and naive. He had done it to make a point, to manipulate the Press and make a statement in a way which I know now he saw as a normal method of expressing himself. The now bloodstained white bandages were rolled down and Richey brandished his arm for the camera, an odd half smile on his face and the stencilled phrase 'Spectators Of Suicide' emblazoned on his shirt across his abdomen. Sometimes when the now legendary photo is published uncropped, you can see me stood to the left of Richey looking disgusted.

The wounds obviously needed stitching and someone mentioned phoning for an ambulance, but Richey didn't want that. Nicky asked me where the nearest hospital was and, as I lived nearby, I directed them there. We trooped outside in subdued silence and waited near the plush minibus that was the band's transport for the tour.

Bizarrely, two groupies were already lurking by the door. We got on the bus and they followed, unchallenged, and sat at the front, to the left of the driver. Sandy and I were handed bottles of Aqua Libra from the band's rider to drink. The Robert De Niro film 'Taxi Driver' was playing on the on-bus video.

NICKY

With my directions we made our way through Norwich city centre. James and Sean wanted to turn in for the night, so we trundled up past the railway station to drop them off first at the modest hotel on the Yarmouth Road where they were staying, stopping off first at the Kentucky Fried Chicken takeaway on Prince Of Wales Road, so they could get some chips.

For most of the journey back through the city centre to Norfolk And Norwich Hospital on Newmarket Road, I tried to ask Richey why he'd done it. By this point, the shock had worn off and I was inexplicably furious with him. It was beyond my comprehension how or why someone could harm themselves in such a way, whatever the reason, and not only hurt himself, but hurt the people who cared about him . A weary looking Nicky shook his head gently at me and said "Just leave it. It's just something he does. You won't understand." And for all the reasons that have become apparent since, I still don't really. When we arrived at the hospital, Nicky helped Richey book into Accident and Emergency and eventually, his small figure was lead off by a nurse. Nicky came back to the waiting room, where we were seated, and sat down heavily.

After offering to buy us hot chocolate from the waiting room's vending machine, he said: "You can do the interview now if you want, while we're waiting." In the context of such a strange evening, I wasn't even remotely surprised that he still wanted to go ahead with it and I got out the little tape recorder I'd borrowed from the student radio station. Sitting there under the flickering fluorescent lights of the waiting room, we talked about all the normal things you talk to bands about in a distant and disaffected manner, about the band's feelings of their home country and much of the stuff they had already talked to Steve Lamacq about. We also talked about the events of that evening, but it was still too recent to register in my mind and make any sense.

After about half an hour, Richey came out of the treatment room. He'd had 17 stitches and the doctor had told him it should heal, but it would probably leave a scar. He had just missed slicing a major vein. Richey remained unperturbed. I said I was sorry for being hard on him, but the night's events had just really thrown me. He said he was sorry, but he really hadn't meant to upset anyone. Nicky said they would drop Sandy and I off, but we decided we needed some fresh air. We walked back to our respective homes in stunned silence.

In the last strange and unbelievable event to come out of that evening, when I got home, the tape I'd used for the interview was completely blank. For whatever reason, human error or mechanical fault, it hadn't recorded a word. It was almost as if there was a strange voodoo hex on the whole night.

After cancelling their planned gig in Birmingham the following night, Richey rang Steve Lamacq apologising for any distress he might have caused.

"You have to put it into the context of where we come from. Back there, people don't believe in bands anyway...the thing for us is, it's really hard to convince you that we are for real. I know you don't like us, but we are for real. When I was a teenager I never had a band who said anything about my life, that's why we're doing this. Where we came from, we had nothing" (Richey, NME, May 1991)

He said later he didn't regret a thing of what he'd done and added: "Other bands hit journalists and it's very macho...I would never want to do that."

This surreal night was my introduction to the Manics, the night which sparked my interest in the band, which is why I've chosen to begin my story about them with my view of that evening's events. But this book is not about me. So let's go back to the beginning.

CHAPTER 02
ARCHIVES OF PAIN

The Manics, as a band, were born in 1989 out of the hills and rain of Wales, a land more well-known musically through history for male voice choirs and Tom Jones. The band later said that the weather there made them what they were, giving them "a feeling of melancholy that drew us together." (Nicky, The Guardian, May 1996).

Now, the misty valleys of Wales have produced a vibrant music scene boasting the likes of Super Furry Animals, Catatonia and Gorky's Zygotic Mynci, which caused The New York Times to proclaim Newport in South Wales the 'new Seattle'. The town's local politician even had a bill passed in the House Of Commons in November 1996 asking that MPs pass a motion acknowledging the fact and commending the bands who had given rise to the article. But back then, it was a different story for the four young working-class friends. They grew up together in Blackwood, Gwent in South Wales, a small depressed mining town - more of a village - with about 1000 inhabitants.

Lead guitarist and singer James Dean Bradfield (born 21/2/69) was named after the iconic

02 "WE GET ON TOO WELL. WE FIT TOO SNUGLY, LIKE A SLIPPER, WE'VE JUST GOT USED TO EACH OTHER." (Sean NME 1991)

1950s film star. It was a lucky escape as he was almost named after his dad's favourite film star at the time Clint Eastwood. For much of his adolescent years, he shared a bedroom with his cousin Sean Moore (born 30/7/70), who was later to become his musical co-writer and drummer with the band. A keen cornet player with the South Wales Jazz Orchestra, he moved in with James aged 13 when his parents split up.

James always wanted to be famous and dreamt of being a world leader like Napoleon, until he discovered The Clash and decided to be a rock star. He loved acting in school plays and sang in the school choir.

Meanwhile, bass guitarist Nicholas Jones (later Nicky Wire, born 20/1/69) was dreaming of being a famous sportsman like Ian Botham, the English cricketer, or pursuing a career in football - he captained the under 16s Welsh team and had trials for Arsenal and the Welsh Youth Team.

Across the street from Nicky, Richard James Edwards (born 22/12/67) lived in a house that had been in his family for nine generations. He was a shy child who was forced to go to church and he told his parents of his first hero when he was 14. It was Bobby Sands, the IRA hunger striker. He grew distant from his father at about this time and went to live with his grandmother for a short time. He had few friends, but he was close to James, Sean and Nicky.

The boys had known each other since their time together at Pontypridd Junior School, but they grew closer together as young teenagers at the Oakdale Comprehensive School when they discovered their shared love of music and began to indulge and encourage each other's obsessions.

As Sean said in an NME interview in 1991, "We get on too well. We fit too snugly, like a slipper, we've just got used to each other." Familiarity like that, where each moulds together to make a whole, takes a very special friendship and a lot of history together.

There was nothing to do in Blackwood. One by one as the boys grew up, the local pits and heavy industry plants were being closed down, producing one of the highest rates of unemployment in the country and making it one of the most deprived towns in Britain. Even the town's one cinema closed when the four friends were in their early teens - so they stayed in their bedrooms "where we could play our records and put on our make-up. We were never particularly victimised for being weird because no one ever saw us." (James, Volume 11)

Soon, they realised their shared dream was to be in a successful pop group. But they knew the odds were stacked against them geographically, particularly as the most famous pop band associated with Wales at the time was earnest long-haired softrockers The Alarm.

As they grew older, the four friends grew ever more into their own little clique which rarely ventured out of doors, except for the odd game of football. "We made no effort to make other friends because we felt so happy." (Nicky, The Guardian, February 1992) Instead of focusing their attentions on other people, their thoughts turned inwards on themselves and they became obsessed with the idea of fame, rather than the other more usual teenage boy activities of girls and getting into trouble.

Even when Nicky had one misguided stab at being a 'normal' rebellious teenager when he helped a friend steal a car during his adolescence, it all went horribly wrong. He fell asleep in the front seat and the next thing he knew a police car had pulled up alongside. He was arrested and charged, but got off with a conditional discharge.

They were even slow starters when it came to girls, with Nicky losing his virginity to a childhood sweetheart when he was at the relatively old age of 18. He ended up marrying her. "Me, Richey and James were the retards when it came to girls and we struggled very hard before we got our first girlfriends. Very, very shy. And most people thought we were gay, so they didn't even bother." (Vox, October 1996) In fact, locals saw the teenage Nicky wandering through town in full make-up and nicknamed him Shirley.

While the boys were going through their adolescence, they had their first taste of the cruelty and unfairness of the real world. In 1986, they saw their local community, which made the majority of its money through coal, brought to its knees by the miners' strike.

02

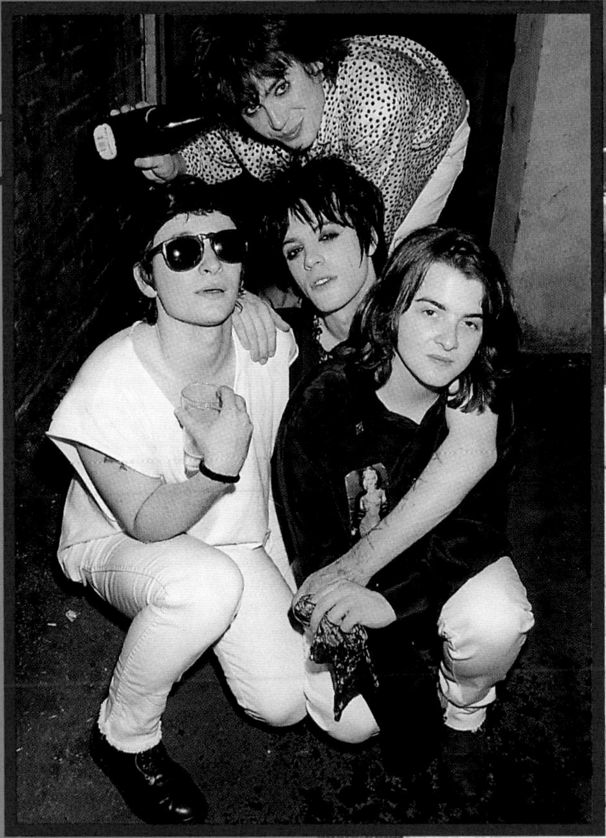

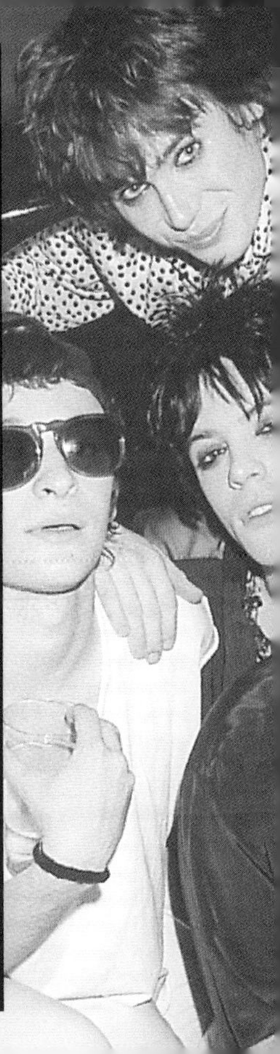

Workers fighting for fairer wages and working conditions were literally starved back to work by the Conservative government of the time that refused to bow to any of their demands. Even when the miners gave up and returned to work, the Government slowly began closing mines down. A black cloud was beginning to descend on South Wales.

At this point, Nicky started writing poetry inspired by the situation and one was put to music and played with James - their first song together. It was, apparently terrible. Nevertheless, despite the bleak economic and social climate pervading Blackwood, the boys still managed to have a generally happy childhood.

James laughed later while reflecting on his youth: "We've always got a kick out of goading people into thinking we were complete tossers. Everyone has their own little gang when they're at school, that's what we're like. We realised as individuals we were very limited as people so we had to fabricate ourselves and took a very academic approach at being a band." (Volume, issue 11)

As a very literary bunch who devoured books, all of them did well at school, Richey and Nicky in particular. After their time at Crosskeys Tertiary College, Richey managed to get three grade As at A level and went on to study history and politics at Swansea University.

Nicky went on to study at Portsmouth Polytechnic. He had gone there because his teachers predicted he would get very low grades in his A-levels. However, his results ended up being much better than anyone had hoped - all As and Bs. But he had a miserable time there and eventually, he persuaded his mother to try and get him into Swansea, where Richey was. His mother telephoned the university and her wheedling worked. They let him in.

When Nicky arrived there to study politics, he was disappointed to discover he had read most of the books on his course already and that his course tutors did not give him the freedom or encouragement to study what he wanted. So in a rather resigned fashion, he came to view his time at university as three years of avoiding getting a proper job and deciding instead what to do with his life.

He spent most of his time shunning the normal student lifestyle. Instead of spending weekends socialising on campus or getting involved with student politics, he retreated home to stay with his parents virtually every weekend. Instead of spending his money on beer like most of his contemporaries, he spent it on fruit machines to the extent that he finished £3000 in debt. He was later to say that he didn't care that much about his financial predicament as he was convinced he would be incredibly rich and famous one day with the band. James helped out his friend by sending the odd £5 or £10 earned from a bar job back home and the pair wrote to each other up to three times a week, as did Richey and Sean. As a result of his disregard for the normal student way of life, Nicky had few friends at university apart from Richey: "We used to go and play golf all the time. Not very rock'n'roll I'm afraid!". The nearest the pair of them got to becoming involved with usual campus activities was when Richey bizarrely painted himself white to dress up as semen for the university's Rag Week.

Richey, who hated his other fellow students, had already got into a pattern of drinking heavily and began fasting as he approached his finals. When he took them, he was below seven stone. He also started cutting himself while revising, using a compass. The behaviour which was later to be ascribed to a rock'n'roll lifestyle had, in fact, started well before Richey even joined the band.

James and Nicky had already done some busking in Cardiff by this point, but they finally decided to embark on their musical odyssey and formed a band called Betty Blue in 1988, together with Sean. Richey, who had just graduated with a 2:1 degree, joined the band as a driver.

But eventually, it was decided that Richey should replace rhythm guitarist Flicker, even though he couldn't really play. He also took over the main lyric writing job, helped out by Nicky, an arrangement that was to continue throughout Richey's time in the band. Nicky moved over to play bass and Richey decided they should change their name to the Manic Street Preachers.

Shortly afterwards, they played their first gig at the Blackwood Little Theatre, followed afterwards by their first London gig at The Horse And Groom in Great Portland Street, where they were rather opportunely seen by then Melody Maker journalist, St Etienne's Bob Stanley. He was taken by this glammed up punk band who emanated outrage and boredom. Even though they had more attitude than musical talent, he decided to interview them for the paper. Full of invective, anger, pride and self-belief, it was to set the pattern for their future excursions in the music press.

The friends scrimped and saved and eventually saved enough money to press up 300 copies of their debut single, 'Suicide Alley' in August 1989. One of the copies was sent to the offices of NME, complete with an impassioned press release written by Richey describing the band as the "suicide of the non-generation." It was made Single Of The Week.

The embryonic band then managed to persuade punky imprint Damaged Goods to release the 'New Art Riot' EP in June 1990, but it didn't make much of an impression on the record buying public.

By the time Nicky had finished his degree in 1990, the band had started gigging around the country. The night before his finals, the band supported The Levellers. As a result, Nicky only got a 2:2, but as he was later to admit, the band were beginning to get noticed so he wasn't too bothered.

Now free from university studies and other diversions, the band concentrated their efforts on making their mark in the industry by diligently rehearsing in the front room of James's house and sending a deluge of letters off to record companies, music papers and press officers asking for help in their career.

With almost religious zeal, they made it their mission to attempt to wake people out of their 20th century slumber, to make music glamorous and interesting again. "We started at a time when rock'n'roll was dead...The UK was in the grip of the dance, rap and the acid house thing. All that Manchester sound stuff that sounded so contrived...We were consciously reacting against all that...we felt we had to do something to bring back rock'n'roll, so that's how the Manic Street Preachers came about." (Richey, Toronto Star, April 1992)

Most music industry types who received one of the Manics "check us out, we're brilliant and we're here to save rock'n'roll" letters dismissed them with a curt "we'll check you out when you come to London. But one such person to receive one of their incendiary Karl Marx-quoting missives along with a copy of 'New Art Riot' was Philip Hall, who became intrigued and offered to see the band if they ever played London.

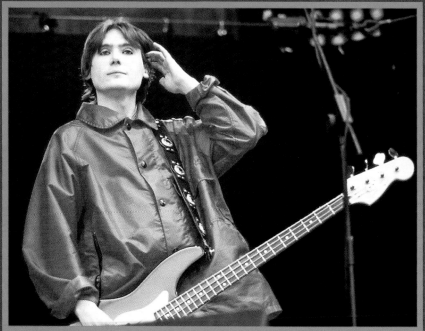

Hall, founder of the London-based management and press company Hall Or Nothing, was managing The Stone Roses and was busy pinning them onto the international map. The band were not really aware of the importance he had in the music industry, but were convinced that he could be the man to send them on their way to success. As it was hardly likely at this stage that they would get to play London again in the immediate future, they eventually persuaded Hall to attend one of their rehearsals at Oakdale Comprehensive School.

Despite the fact that they still couldn't play their instruments properly, Hall could see the band had potential and that any lack of musical talent was more than made up for by the band's conviction and belief in what they were doing, helped along by the androgynous, glamorous image and their intellect.

What is more, he could see how well the band functioned as a unit. They felt that they had power together rather than individually, with each making up for each other's inefficiencies - there was Nicky, the handsome one, Richey, the articulate, sensitive one, Sean "brutality personified", according to James, and himself? "A bit musical and a bit of a lad."

As Mandi James said in the CD magazine Volume 11, "The Manics are saying things people haven't said for a long time in a way people haven't said them...they've tapped into the psyche of fucked-up adolescence, communicating alienation and despair through vicious soundbites and hair-raising riffs."

02

Hall's imagination was caught instantly. So he became their publicist and co-manager with his brother Martin and three months later, he moved the band to West London where they kipped down on the floor of his house which he shared with wife Terri. They stayed there for more than six months, but Hall was completely committed to his new charges and even remortgaged his house to loan them £45,000 to keep them in food and clothes while they searched for a record deal.

The Manics decided that Heavenly was the most happening label around at that time, so they set about trying to win the heart of the label's owner, Jeff Barrett.

Barrett was already familiar with the band through the pages of London fanzine Hungry Beat, which the band would often contribute to, so they could basically rant about themselves, about how they wanted to rage against the ordinary, sell 20 million records and self-destruct..

Jeff recalled later of his first encounter: "I was handed this letter and told 'read this'. It was passionate,

> **"I WAS HANDED THIS LETTER AND TOLD 'READ THIS'. IT WAS PASSIONATE, ON FIRE, IT WANTED TO CHANGE THE WORLD AND IT REALLY EXCITED ME. UNFORTUNATELY, THEIR DEMO TAPE DIDN'T DO AS MUCH FOR ME."**

on fire, it wanted to change the world and it really excited me. Unfortunately, their demo tape didn't do as much for me."

But then three years later, he was presented with 'Motown Junk'. He went to see the band play a gig at London's Rock Garden in August 1990 and couldn't resist. Heavenly released the record on January 21 1991. 'Motown Junk' was the starting point for us really. That was the first time we ever really felt like a band, the first time we created a record we could live with. We had people around us who understood exactly what we were trying to say and how we wanted to say it..." (James, Volume 11)

The record was made the NME's Single Of The Week. In March 1991, the band had played their first overseas gig at the Paris Locomotive Club with Flowered Up, East Village and St Etienne as part of a

Heavenly showcase tour. Just after that, they embarked on a tour of Ireland. NME journalist James Brown accompanied them and afterwards wrote up the first real in-depth interview with the band that had appeared in the music press. In the resulting feature, Nicky revealed that Richey had a sleepwalking problem. This was to escalate later into full-scale insomnia, the cure for which Richey sought in the bottom of bottles of whatever alcohol was to hand.

The band were in full sneering anarchist-Situationist guise at the time, intent on being as high-profile as Guns'n'Roses while being as in-yer-face as Public Enemy, the Manics two favourite bands. Richey was busy writing Situationist manifestos, while Nicky cut out photos of Marilyn Monroe to stick to shirts bought from Miss Selfridge to wear for their gigs.

Their music and live shows brought to mind a hybrid mixture of The New York Dolls, Nicky - Stiff Little Fingers and The Clash, with an often be-frocked Nicky scissor-kicking around the stage, Richey doing his best Keith Richards impression, Sean bashing hell out of his drum kit and James yowling like a man possessed. The passion and energy was infectious and often sparked riotous behaviour in the audience, who would respond by throwing beer and moshing violently. Off stage, the band were just as arrogant, proud and mouthy, proclaiming to anyone who listened their vehement dislike of the British Royal Family, The Stone Roses, Shaun Ryder and conversely, their love of Andy Warhol, Kevin Rowland, Aleister Crowley, The Who, Bob Marley, Led Zeppelin, The Faces, and Sega Megadrive. They broadcast their love of literature and would cite favourite writers including Camus, Rimbaud, Dante, Socrates, Sylvia Plath and Bret Easton Ellis. A bundle of contradictions from the start, these rather high-brow interests were also coupled with a more low-brow healthy appetite for no-ties sex with groupies. But though they held up such dualities for public scrutiny, they made no apologies. Love them or hate them, you couldn't ignore them which was

MANICS

exactly what they wanted. They revelled in the notoriety and delighted in being confrontational.

The band were full of opinions on anything put to them, whether it was the IRA or the monarchy. Most of their venom, however, was saved for the music press who they felt had betrayed them. Where once papers like NME and Melody Maker were the only publications they cared for, now music journalists branded them "revivalist fakers". They did not take kindly to being labelled sloganeering media prostitutes, of aping bands who have gone before them, or having their idealism questioned or their agendas belittled.

Richey hit back with "Rock'n'roll has become a repetitive lifestyle - everybody lives out what's gone in the past. We're all about second-hand ideas. What else can you do?" (Richey, NME)

However, the band managed to convince sceptical scribe Brown with their gig on the final night of their Irish tour in Dublin, a 30 minute blast of pure adrenaline when Nicky injured his foot tearing around the stage and Richey smashed his guitar through the roof of the venue after the anti-love song vitriol of 'Motown Junk'.

As journalist Andrew Smith of The Times said, they were a band ahead of their time. They wanted to rail against the apathy of the time, as embodied by the outgoing shoegazing scene and the still strong baggy movement. "Manic Street Preachers wanted nothing more than to rain on that summer of pills and hippie-dippie platitudes. In effect they were their generations' Sex Pistols..." (Andrew Smith, The Times, May 1996)

But all this attention wasn't enough and on May 11 the band decided to sign to Columbia, one of the labels belonging to the huge Sony corporation, which was ironically home of The Clash, one of the Manic's favourite bands and one with which they were often compared. The deal was worth £250,000 plus £400,000 to record their first album.

Heavenly's Jeff Barrett was not overjoyed by their decision at the time, having only just acquired his ungrateful new young charges. James explained their decision later. "You don't have a dream so you can cut out little faded pieces from fanzines all your life. You want glossy stuff that's not going to fade. We always wanted to reach as many people as possible." (Volume, issue 11) Barrett, however, could understand

02

The lyrics to 'You Love Us', with its vitriolic contempt for modern society, also gave a subtext that said they wanted to live fast, die young and leave a beautiful corpse, matching the zeitgeist of the '4Real' incident.

Writer Caitlin Moran shared the opinions of many people, male and female, when she described Richey as "the most untouchably beautiful person I have ever seen in my life" when she first met him 1992. She gushed: "His hair has that 'rockstar' glow. His skin is translucent and punctured only by two huge, soft-brown Bambi eyes. He has the kind of bone structure that would make Kate Moss's agent weep." (The Times, October 1994)

By now, the band had become quite the media darlings, real rock stars, with national newspapers as well as the established music press beating a path to their door. The Richey incident, complete with their soundbite slogans like 'Destroy Work' and 'London Death Sentence' and 'Waste '91' had Fleet Street journalists alternately enthralled and repulsed.

The band hit the headlines shortly afterwards following a near riot when they played one of the Cambridge University May Balls, when Sean trashed his drum kit and James hit a member of the audience after just four songs. It set a trend and much of the early Manics gigs were filled with crowdbaiting, which often provoked a hail of beer glasses and bodies flinging themselves offstage over the heads of the front row of the audience. The band released their first single for Columbia 'Stay Beautiful' in July 1991, and their media profile was further enhanced when it made the top 40, their first chart hit.

During a show at Reading later that summer, their show had to be stopped after six songs as the stage descended into a chaos of bodies, bouncers and beer zigzagging in front of the band, who began to fight with members of the audience.

As Martin Aston commented in The Independent, "Coming after a glut of noise-fixated guitar bands who stare at their effects pedals, Manic Street Preachers are like the first signs of spring..." (The Independent, August 1991)their reasoning, and remains good friends with the band to this day.

Four days after the Manics signed to Columbia, they released their second single for Heavenly 'You Love Us', which became yet another NME Single Of The Week. On the same day, Richey carved the words '4Real' into his forearm at the Norwich Arts Centre. Afterwards, there were huge rows in the offices of NME as to whether the photographs of his arm, taken by Ed Sirrs, should be published.

Some staff thought it was sick and disgusting, others could understand why Richey had done the deed. Former NME writer James Brown, who is now editor of Loaded magazine, was more forthright in his views, and said: "We've got to print that. It's rock'n'roll, innit? I think more bands should do that sort of thing. It's artistic expression." Brown's arguments won the day and the photo was reproduced in full colour in the paper. A recording of the debate was later to appear on the B-side of the Manics' cover of 'Theme From M*A*S*H (Suicide Is Painless)'.

Many national daily newspaper editors shared Brown's view and Richey made headlines in papers throughout Britain.

What is more, teenagers throughout Britain had suddenly discovered someone who felt as inwardly tortured as themselves. Here was someone who was articulating their hurt and alienation at the world around them. The Manics were beginning to achieve their aim of being the spokesmen for a lost generation.

"THERE IS ELOQUENCE IN SCREAMING." (Patrick Jones, from the sleevenotes of the Manic's LP 'Generation Terrorists')

CHAPTER **03**
GENERATION TERRORISM

In January 1992, with the reissue of 'You Love Us', the band reached a landmark in their career with their first appearance on Top Of The Pops, an ideal opportunity for a band who wanted to subvert by utilising the mainstream.

The Manics continued to define their image as the beautiful rebels of rock'n'roll when their debut album 'Generation Terrorists' hit the shops on February 10 1992, a pungent aural punch filled with vim, vigour and spleen, which Nicky hoped would achieve the band's ambition of being "nailed to history as soon as we can". Richey, by his own proud admission, did not play a note on it, but contributed the lyrics of revolution, self-loathing and railing against the world .

A statement on a grand scale filled with political and literary references, the double album - described by one critic as a Situationist soap opera - also gave a contradictory message about the Manics. If they really wanted to rebel, why was it filled with conventional-sounding hit pop singles like 'Motorcycle Emptiness'? And the same old question of why on a major label?

Richey had the answer. "The whole indie mentality that grew up from punk onwards just seemed so bullshit to us because the most subversive really important group in the world were Public Enemy, and they were on Columbia. The level of corruption on an indie label is just on a smaller scale." To them, four working class boys from Blackwood who society

03

GENERATION
TERRORISTS

dictated should have no rosy future, success was their rebellion against the world and they were going to get there on their own terms. And what better way to convey their very serious messages than by using accessible music as a conductor?

Their rather startling intent at the time was to sell 20 million copies of their debut album and then split up. That could hardly be achieved unless the music was populist. They even surprised the establishment by getting ex-porn star Traci Lords to sing on 'Little Baby Nothing', which was to become a hit in January 1994. They wanted her or Kylie Minogue, two women who had always been perceived by the media as patriarchally-manipulated puppets, so they could show they lived by their own agendas.

It all added up to overwhelm critics and music lovers everywhere and the album went gold and eventually spawned six top 40 hits.

The first of these was 'Slash 'N' Burn', which went straight into the Top 20 in March.

In May, the band released 'Motorcycle Emptiness', their paen against Thatcherism, which also charted. That month, the band embarked on their first US tour.

During that tour, NME's Stuart Bailie, who was interviewing the band, could not help but be transfixed by Richey's self-inflicted scars. "You start looking at his right arm; burns, scrapes, slices, lesions - a lurid pink testimony to a sustained programme of self-abuse." But Richey defended himself by saying: "They're just my war wounds. I've always found it hard to express how I feel, even from when I was a little child. It's a very British emotion - they keep things bottled up inside them. Some more than others." (NME, May 1992)

The Manics got a further rung up the ladder of pop success when they played the main stage of the Reading Festival that August in front of 40,000 people, where they debuted their cover of 'Suicide Is Painless', the theme tune of the American pathos tinged comedy show set during the Korean war. The month afterwards, the band went into a Cardiff studio and recorded it for the charity compilation 'Ruby Trax' celebrating NME's 40th birthday. It took them just a day, at a cost of £80, and was described at the time as "an epic just waiting for the Manic Street Preachers to cover it." (October 3, NME)

The band had chosen it as it reminded them of a gloomy time in their lives when there was a Musician's

Union strike so there was hardly any music on TV at all.

It went on to become the band's first top 10 success in the UK, an achievement that left the band ironically nonplussed, considering their dreams of chart domination.

When asked how they felt about reaching such a milestone in their careers, they said they "couldn't really care less", they were just glad to be making money for the Spastics Society.

But the Manics are never far away from controversy and contradictions and Nicky managed to diminish their humanitarian image somewhat in December that year when they played the London Kilburn National. In an outburst that caused a public outcry, Nicky, in a somewhat drunken state, exclaimed that he hoped REM lead singer Michael Stipe would "go the same way as Freddie Mercury", who had been lead singer of Queen and had recently died of AIDS.

He later apologised and the real reason behind his illogical and unpleasant outburst was revealed - the Manic's manager Philip Hall was dying of cancer and the hostile tirade had been a result of his misplaced anguish of watching his demise.

1993 began as a year in which the Manics felt they could really achieve something, especially when they released their second album 'Gold Against The Soul' in June.

The band were beginning to see some of the financial rewards of all their years of hard work following their chart success and the album had been recorded in a lush studio, replete with swimming pools, that cost the band a staggering £2000 a day to hire.

Although the band now claim to despise the album, it proved that the band could create heart-stopping anthems like 'La Tristesse Durera' ('This sadness will go on'), named after artist Van Gogh's last words,

> "LIKE A LEAF IN THE AUTUMN BREEZE/LIKE A FLOOD IN JANUARY/WE DON'T WANT YOUR FUCKING LOVE" (lyrics to single 'Roses In The Hospital')

and 'Life Becoming A Landslide' which sounded like it had been made for stadium play and mass adoration, while still emoting the pain of disillusioned youth.

Filled with killer riffs, heartfelt, bittersweet lyrics dealing with drugs, mental illness and war, expressed through well-crafted melodies, the Manics had proved they were no flash in the punk pop pan. Singles 'La Tristesse Durera' and 'Roses In The Hospital' were again successful, but the band were to be dealt a bitter blow.

On December 7 1993, the band's co-manager, publicist and mentor Philip Hall died after a lengthy battle with cancer. The band, who had looked upon him as a father figure, were devastated.

"Philip was the first person that understood us. He was more than a manager, and his input into the band was invaluable. Without his help, motivation and generosity, it is doubtful whether we as a band, would have carried on." (Manic's statement to NME, December 1993)

By the time the year ended, Richey's drinking problems had escalated and he was drinking more than half a bottle of vodka a day, finished off with 40 cigarettes.

"I KNOW I BELIEVE IN NOTHING. BUT IT IS MY NOTHING." (Richey, 1994)

CHAPTER 04
BECOMING A LANDSLIDE

1994 was, according to NME, "The Year That Rock Cracked Up" and the Manics copped more than their fair share of the malaise.

Rather than dealing with their grief at the loss of Philip Hall, they suppressed their emotions by simply going straight out on tour.

In one of the Manics' first interviews of the year, Richey already seemed to be having bad vibes about it. "Nobody ever goes, 'I feel great, life's treated me fine.' It's the classic thing having an industrial society where most people absorb things their grandparents would never have dreamed of and there's just a massive general air of disillusionment." (The Times, January 1994)

However, by this time, he was making a concerted effort to learn to play guitar, which boded well for his future in the band and they started off 1994 releasing a new single 'Life Becoming A Landslide' on January 31. Melody Maker screamed "It's 1994 and the Manic Street Preachers are the only band that matters".

Richey continued to speak of his fear of not being able to sleep, telling journalist David Bennun "I get paranoid about not being able to sleep. And if by eight o'clock I haven't had a drink, I get massive panic attacks and I'll be awake all night, and that's my biggest nightmare. I can't stomach that thought. That's why I drink. It's a very simple choice. By about midday I need a drink to stabilise me." (January,

Melody Maker) Perhaps the insomnia was caused by the horrors of the world that came back to haunt him when he shut his eyes.

In March, Richey's best friend at university hung himself. The pair had shared a flat and this death simply compounded the grief Richey was already suffering from the death of Philip Hall.

On the other side of the Atlantic in April that year, Kurt Cobain, lead singer of US grunge band Nirvana, shot himself, leaving a note saying it was better to "burn out than fade away".

It was yet another death to affect the band, especially Richey, and shortly afterwards the band undertook a week long tour of Thailand, which Nicky later cited as one of the turning points in Richey's depression.

The lyricist had become a whirl of contradictions, on one hand slamming on about how the country's economy was built on sex and abuse of the young then on the other paying a prostitute to give him a hand job. During their stay there, Richey was also given a set of knives by a young Thai fan who apparently told him to look at her when he cut himself with them. Since the moment they had stepped onto Thai soil, the band had been pestered by fans asking them to autograph photos of Richey's self-mutilated arms. He duly obliged the obsessives' strange bloodlust and later made use of his new gift offstage, scoring his chest with the blades. Ever the soft, bruised puppy behind the posturing rock star exterior, it is hardly surprising that knowing Richey's psychological make-up, he channelled his fears into such a physical sign of distress.

After the tour, the band took a holiday in Portugal but it did not improve Richey's condition. He started crying involuntarily. His mental state deteriorated and when the band returned from their holiday, Richey locked himself away in his flat for two days on a self-mutilation binge.

His grief in losing two people close to him in such a short space of time had magnified his insomnia, which in turn compounded his problems with alcohol and he admitted he was now drinking a bottle of vodka a night to try and help himself sleep.

RICHEY

In July, Richey voluntarily admitted himself to a Whitchurch Hospital in Cardiff where he stayed for eight days in the psychiatric ward. It was hell. Lumped in with schizophrenics and all manner of mentally disturbed people, Richey was simply drugged up with the anti-depressant Librium and left alone. The band described it as being a "flotation tank for people who can't cope".

At this point, Richey even asked the band if he could leave to just write their lyrics, and give up performing altogether, though he later changed his mind.

Three weeks after, it was announced that Richey had been hospitalised with nervous exhaustion, a term which incorporated his alcoholism, anorexia, insomnia, self-mutilation and depression after his non-appearance at the Manic's gig at Glasgow's T In The Park music festival.

Richey's family, the management and the rest of the band had rescued him and moved him to the £300-a-day Priory Hospital in Roehampton, South London, previously used by the likes of Shaun Ryder. There, Richey was put on the 12-step programme, used by addiction support groups like Alcoholics Anonymous. Richey also joined the AA while he was there. Nicky felt Roehampton could have made Richey's problems even worse. "They say they've got a cure in places like that but all they do is completely change the person you are...they ripped the soul out of him. The person I knew was slowly ebbing away. I think he knew that too." (Nicky, The Times, May 1996)

Richey's illness had come as no surprise to the rest of the Manics. The band knew their friend was depressed as he had never tried to hide it from them and in turn they had tried their best to look out for him. But his problems were deeper than even they had realised.

The warning signs had become apparent during an interview that Richey had given MTV at the NME Brat Awards at the beginning of the year.

"The older you get, the more life becomes miserable. All the people you grew up with die. Your parents die, your dog dies, your energy diminishes."

The band launched their new single 'Revol' in August while Richey was still recovering, described antagonistically by Nicky thus: "This song is not about revolution and it's not about fucking S*M*A*S*H and it's got fuck all to do with The Family Cat." (Melody Maker, August 1994)

Later that month, as the Manics were preparing to launch their third album 'The Holy Bible' on their new label Epic, which was also owned by Sony, Nicky revealed that Richey might not be able to join their UK tour that autumn. The tour was due to begin at Glasgow's Barrowlands on October 5, but the band decided that if Richey was not well enough, they would rather go ahead as a trio than get someone to replace him. The band said they would play the Reading Festival that month as a three-piece and see how they felt after that. After all, they had only played one gig before without Richey and they had hated every minute.

It's hard to believe that some people thought Richey's breakdown was a faked-up stunt to get more publicity for the new album, and the band's poignant performance at Reading on the anniversary of Philip Hall's birthday was made all the more saddening by the absence of Richey. Some music journalists described it being as icy and despairing as a wake. They followed their performance with four more pre-arranged dates as a trio and rumours abounded that the band would split. "I think a lot of groups would have got in another guitarist for those five dates but that wouldn't have been right for us," James told Stuart Maconie in Q at the time. "To be honest, we were all numb to any sort of discussion about the group's future because we were too concerned about Richey. We've grown up together. He's a friend first and foremost...It would have been a betrayal...." (James, Q Oct 1994)

On August 30, the band released their third album, 'The Holy Bible', which emerged as a sombre and bleak affair, mirroring Richey's increasingly worrying mental state during the course of 1994. Nicky admitted at the time it was "quite a morbid album" (Nicky, Melody Maker, August 1994) To reflect the mood, the band had recorded the album in a seedy studio in the red-light area of Cardiff as opposed to the lush surrounds where they recorded 'Gold Against The Soul' to get a more "honest" sound. Though crammed full as ever with social and political rhetoric, the band's third album was more personal than any of their previous work, as if Richey, the main lyricist, had been taking stock of his life and the band's success. Even the cover, a triptych called 'Strategy (South/Front Face/North Face)' of an enormously fat woman painted by acclaimed artist Jenny Saville, seemed to symbolise the band's state of mind. Naked but for her bra and pants, she regards the reflection of her body in an intent but contemptuous manner. The triptych is eerily mirrored on the cover of band's following album 'Everything Must Go', their first recorded since Richey's disappearance. But instead of the views of the unnamed woman, it is of the three remaining members of the band, poignantly used at half the size of Jenny Saville's art work, as if the remaining Manics feel half a band without Richey.

The most issue-led album that the Manics had recorded, 'The Holy Bible' was also a powerful and painful depiction of Richey's preoccupations at the time, the horror of the world around him and within his head. Once Richey had written the majority of the claustrophobic and resonant lyrics, helped by Nicky, the band sat around and formulated the album in what James described as an almost academic manner, so that each song was "like an essay," with James and Sean moulding the musical shape. It is no great shock then that each and every one of the tracks have since been pulled to pieces and analysed for clues as to Richey's later disappearance.

'Yes' draws analogies between how society views prostitutes and how the Manics felt they had prostituted themselves over the preceding years, selling their souls for fame. Other songs deal with American consumerism as opposed to British imperialism ('Ifwhiteamericatoldthetruthforonedayitsworldwouldfallapart') and the idea that men are a genetic aberration on 'Of Walking Abortion', which mentions the Hungarian fascist military dictator Horthy. "You're never going to eradicate all the evils of the world, but I do think the horror of ourselves is 95 per cent confined to men and it's men who've got to change - they are the perpetrators of 95 per cent of the world's violent crimes...Men are the beasts of the race, the fucks of the world." (Nicky, Vox, October 1996)

The band further courted controversy with 'Archives Of Pain', which derides the glorification of serial killers. Named after a chapter in a book by deconstructionist theorist Michel Foucault, which calls for punishment to fit the crime, many saw the song as an extremely right wing pro-capital punishment song. James claimed the band did not necessarily hold such right-wing views, and though they were not left-wing either, the song simply showed how confused and hypocritical modern times and the band themselves were. Nicky said more

MANICS

simply "it's just against this fascination with people who kill. A lot of people don't like to see rapists getting off with a £25 fine." (Nicky, Melody Maker August 1994)

Other issues include freedom of speech and political correctness ('PCP'), concentration camps, the Holocaust and the reality of war ('Mausoleum' and 'The Intense Humming Of Evil'), yearning for the innocence of childhood ('This Is Yesterday') and the failure of relationships ('Revol').

Arguably, the most personal song on the album is '4st 7lbs', about the so-called slimmers' disease anorexia nervosa, with lyrics including: "I don't mind the horror that surrounds me/Self-worth scatters, self-esteem's a bore/I long since moved to a higher plateau/this discipline's so rare/...such beautiful dignity in self-abuse."

"Every word of that is Richey's and it's pretty autobiographical. I think that when he was admitted to hospital, he was down to about six stones, which, for a five-foot-eight 25 year old, is pretty grim." (Nicky, Melody Maker, August 1994)

Others strong hints to Richey's mental state are provided in 'Faster', in which Richey alludes to his self-mutilation - "I am an architect/They call me a butcher" and 'Die In The Summertime' where Richey likens himself to "A tiny animal curled into a quarter circle" and gives a graphically disturbing insight into his self-abuse: "Scratch my leg with a rusty nail/Sadly it heals/...I wanna die, die in the summertime". 'She Is Suffering' describes the very Buddhist idea of ridding the body of desire to achieve internal peace and harmony.

When released in October 1994, it became the band's 14th top 40 single, but despite the trauma of the year theband were still not being complacent about their pop status. It still wasn't enough. "We're known in Britain, Japan, Thailand, we've had hits in Holland. But this is our third album and we've only played six fucking gigs in America. That's got to stop. We're still in love with the idea of The Beatles kissing the tarmac at JFK. We're still in love with the word 'million'." (James, Q October 1994)

"I THINK THAT WHEN HE WAS ADMITTED TO HOSPITAL, HE WAS DOWN TO ABOUT SIX STONES, WHICH, FOR A FIVE-FOOT-EIGHT 25 YEAR OLD, IS PRETTY GRIM." (Nicky, Melody Maker, August 1994)

Luckily, Richey recovered enough for the band's autumn UK tour and to warm up, they went on an 11-date tour as support for Irish rock band Therapy?. However, his demons had only been suppressed rather than exorcised. The band's management gave strict instructions to the press not to talk to Richey in an attempt to keep him out of the public gaze. But his mental turbulence was always bubbling under the surface.

While in Bordeaux that September, James said "He has wanted to cut himself on this tour already, but hasn't. And that's a first. We're taking things slowly. He knows he can leave the band whenever he wants, whenever it gets too much...If he left, the band would probably be over. I can't imagine the Manics without him". (The Times, October 1994)

Richey had written a quote from feminist Andrea Dworkin on his set list reading: "I also had nightmares. Somehow all the feelings I didn't feel when each thing had actually happened to me I did feel when I slept." Despite his troubles, Caitlin Moran said of his performance that night: "Onstage he simultaneously embodies and supersedes the role of rockstar; his interpretation is definitive, brilliantly observed, played out in full and heartfelt and, in having studied his subject so well he a) becomes a Master In Iconography - and therefore an icon himself - and b) proves the whole art form redundant; he highlights the weaknesses in a career which will be, in the end, a couple of gold discs on the wall and a clutch of laminates slung around the bedroom doorknob" (October 1994) Perhaps Richey himself had already begun to think in such a way, to slip into the trap of questioning the futility of his existence, of any existence.

At the beginning of their headlining UK tour the following month, all eyes were on Richey, the "alcoholic anorexic wearing a scar tissue suit from years of self-abuse." (Ryan Gilbey, The Independent, October 1994). This time, at their opening date at the Glasgow Barrowlands, Richey scribbled a Shelly quote on his set list: "When will you return the glory of your prime?/No more/Oh, never more!". The band did their best to ignore the skewed focus of attention and continually played tight, aggressive and vigorous sets as Richey went through the motions of pouting, preening and threatening- and occasionally managing to smash his guitar on stage. But that didn't mean he had left his troubles behind him. As Gilbey surmised: "...there was always a sense that the Manics were teetering on the brink of personal apocalypse. Delivered from that brink, there's more urgency about them now, as though they're playing over a trap-door which could spring open at any moment." (The Independent, October 1994) The band did a cover version of Nirvana's 'Penny Royal Tea' which further added an edge to Richey's on stage appearance, given that many people had already plotted a place for Richey alongside Kurt Cobain in the rock'n'roll graveyard.

In fact, Richey's condition was worsening again. He was still following the 12-point plan taught to him at The Priory, but had taken to reading them out loud constantly, so that they began to sound like a mantra. It unnerved the rest of the band.

By the time they embarked on a UK tour in October, Richey had started identifying with the character that Dennis Hopper played of a mad photojournalist in the film 'Apocalypse Now.' Richey even bought the same model of camera that Hopper used in the movie and took to wearing it around his neck, and wearing odd clothes, like tight women's leggings. He then began writing LOVE on the knuckles of his hand.

When the band went on tour with Suede in the November, Richey had become fascinated with Def Leppard guitarist Steve Clarke, who was so nervous before live shows that he once deliberately broke his knuckles on a bathroom sink so that he wouldn't have to play one night. Richey used to fantasise about chopping off his fingers, so he went and bought a butcher's meat cleaver. At a gig in Amsterdam, Nicky discovered that Richey had carved a vertical wound down his upper torso. After a gig in Hamburg, Nicky found Richey outside their hotel headbutting a wall as blood poured down his cheeks.

But the band finished the year in a lighter mood with three life-affirming gigs at the London Astoria on December 19, 20 and 21. The crowd sang "Here we are now: entertain us!" from the Nirvana song 'Smells Like Teen Spirit' at the start of each night. James even donned a Christmas hat to sing a solo cover of Art Garfunkel's rabbit song 'Bright Eyes'. NME's Mark Sutherland noted "As a band, they may bring more

more baggage with them than Ivana Trump on a month's Inter-rail holiday, but away from Richey's traumas and Nicky's open-mouth-insert-both-feet pronouncements, they are more than capable of existing as 'simply' a rock'n'roll spectacle. And a pretty bloody amazing one at that." (Sutherland, NME January 1995)

The verdict was sealed when Richey took centre stage at the end of the last gig and smashed his guitar and amp, with Nicky following suit. Richey then threw himself into Sean's drum kit, Sean started trashing the stage lights and James threw his guitar on stage splitting it in two. The band left the stage one by one to leave Richey alone before the audience thwacking himself on the head with a broken mic stand. £10,000 worth of equipment gleefully trashed.

That Christmas, Richey stopped drinking and was practising his guitar. Maybe, his family thought, he was finally beginning to cope with his problems. Maybe he was on the mend after all. But then one night when the band had gathered together to watch a video, Richey proceeded to pointedly scoff down two whole bars of chocolate in broad view of the others, classic anorexic behaviour. The band took that as a sign that he was still "fucked up."

Looking back on 1994, James said it had been a "drama queen" 12 months, a "bag of shit". But despite the trials and tribulations, they had reached a new maturity. Richey had bought a flat in Cardiff, Nicky had got married, Sean was living with his girlfriend and James had moved out of his parents home and got his own flat in London.

"I discovered the art of switching off. Which I do by enjoying myself...I only go out and get blasted when I've finished work. I'm more professional now. And the band have changed." (James, Select January 1995)

CHAPTER 05
UNCERTAIN TIMES

The band started off 1995 in positive fashion, rehearsing for five days at a secluded studio in Surrey in preparation for recording songs for the soundtrack to the Sylvester Stallone film 'Judge Dredd'. Richey was in unusually good spirits. At the end of their stint there, Richey bought little gifts for his bandmates, The Daily Telegraph and a Mars bar for Nicky, a CD for James, something personal for Sean. And for all of them, he handed over a bundle of latest lyrics he had been working on beforehand.

But in mid-January, Richey went missing for a couple of days. His beloved 14-year-old springer spaniel Snoopy had died and he went awol with grief. When he returned, he had shaved his head and started to wear concentration camp-style pyjamas.

Just afterwards, he gave his last interview, to Midori Tsukagoshi of Japanese magazine Music Life where he talked about how upset he was about the death of his dog and of his unrequited love for an unnamed girl.

Nine days later he went missing. It was on February 1st 1995, the day before James and Richey were due to fly out on a US promotional tour in preparation for the band's planned 36-date tour there later that month, their first since May 1992. But Richey

UNCERTAIN TIMES

checked out of the Embassy Hotel, in Bayswater, London at 7am. In his room, number 516, he left a packed suitcase, his anti-depression drug Prozac and toiletries. There was also a box containing books, a photo, some collages and videos of the Peter Shaffer play Equis and Mike Leigh's Naked wrapped up with literary quotes scribbled on the side, together with a hand-written note that said simply "I love you," for a 19-year-old girl called Jo, who Richey had known for a few years. Both note and package were given to her afterwards.

The band's manager Martin Hall spent February 1 frantically contacting friends and family to see if they had seen Richey, but no-one had. He cancelled the tour and went to Harrow Police Station and reported Richey as missing the next day. He then went to Blackwood and together with Richey's father, searched Richey's flat. Papers were found that indicated Richey had indeed been there since leaving his London hotel, but there were no further clues. He had also left his passport, credit cards and more Prozac.

Richey's parents Sherry and Graham had last seen him on January 23 and had last spoken to him on January 31. According to his father Graham: "There seemed to be nothing wrong. He was looking forward to going." (Western Mail, March 31 1995)

Nevertheless, on February 3, his family placed an advert in the local newspaper saying: "Richard, please make contact. Love, Mum, Dad and Rachel."

Hall Or Nothing, the band's management company, even hired a private investigator, but despite an extensive search of hospitals, airports, ferry terminals and hotels nothing was revealed.

All that could be ascertained was that for the 10 days prior to his disappearance, Richey had withdrawn £200 a day from his bank account.

There were some potential leads shortly after his disappearance.

On February 5, 19-year-old college student David Cross allegedly spoke to Richey at Newport Bus Station. They spoke briefly about a mutual friend, American Manics fan Lori Fiddler, who runs the US Manics fan club.

David maintains he said to Richey: "Hello, Richey, I'm a friend of Lori's." He replied: "How is she? How is she doing?". After that, he said he would see David later and wandered off. David remains positive it was Richey.

More bizarrely, on February 7 at 7am, a Newport taxi driver, Tony Hatherall, picked up a young man from the King's Hotel in Newport. The man, who did not give his name and who had no luggage, got in the car and asked if he could lay down on the back seat. He then gave the bemused and suspicious driver £40 and said he was looking for his boss, who was the manager of a haulage firm and who had broken down somewhere in South Wales. Hatherall was directed to Blackwood bus station, but when they got there, his passenger said it was not the right place and asked to go back to Newport. On the way, he asked to stop off at Pontypool railway station so he could make a telephone call, even though there is no public telephone at the station. When he got back in the car, he asked to be taken to Aust service station near the Severn Bridge, but avoiding all motorways. He was duly taken there via minor roads and dropped off at the bridge, a well-known place for suicides. The fare was £68. Hatherall recalled the mystery man had been talking with a false London accent which he occasionally slipped to reveal a Welsh accent. Once he heard the reports about Richey's disappearance, he also informed the police, but the man he described had long hair, not the shaven scalp that Richey had at the time.

The police eventually went public on February 15. They issued a statement which said: "Richard's family, band members and friends are concerned for his safety and welfare and stress that no pressure would be put on him to return if he does not wish to. They stress that his privacy will be respected at all times."Hall Or Nothing issued another statement which said: "Richard's family, the band and the management are unavailable for comment and we would like to ask you to respect their privacy and for your help and sensitivity regarding this matter."

Two days afterwards, on February 17, Richey's silver L-registration Vauxhall Cavalier car was found at Aust services, where Hatherall had dropped off his mystery man. A car park attendant reported it had been parked there since February 14, St Valentine's Day. Nothing was found in the car to give police any clues to its owners whereabouts. However, the car battery was flat, leading police to believe that perhaps Richey had slept rough in the car over a period of time and had run down the battery playing tapes and using the car heater to keep warm.

"RICHARD'S FAMILY, THE BAND AND THE MANAGEMENT ARE UNAVAILABLE FOR COMMENT AND WE WOULD LIKE TO ASK YOU TO RESPECT THEIR PRIVACY AND FOR YOUR HELP AND SENSITIVITY REGARDING THIS MATTER."

Since then, reported sightings have come from places as far afield as Cambridge, Liverpool, Brighton and Whitby. Some rumours insist he is living in a monastery or ensconced in a remote Welsh Valley. Richey's sister Rachel had in fact written to every monastery she could track down asking if her brother was staying there. Each wrote back saying they couldn't tell her even if he was.

In May 1995, a German friend of Richey's Monika Pommer claimed she had received a postcard from him dated London, February 3, which sent his greetings. She refused to send the card to police investigating his disappearance because she said it was too personal. Instead, she sent a photocopy of a postcard he had sent her previously as proof.

Another reported sighting came in June at Skipton, North Yorkshire, where 16-year-old Lucy Winter said she saw the singer looking "haggard and ill." She told police afterwards: "I had a good look at him and still think it's him."

Following his disappearance, music papers such as Melody Maker and NME were inundated with letters from distraught fans, some gruesomely written in blood and often accompanied with lurid photos of the damage they were inflicting to themselves while they pined for their lost hero.

Letters poured in from anorexics, bulimics and cutters who had taken Richey as their hero, the only one who truly understood them, that shared their secret. There had never been anyone to represent them, their problems had always been hidden before. Yet Richey had repaid their devotion by deserting them and they were distracted with grief. Many made parallels with the suicide of Kurt Cobain in 1994, whose death Richey had been fascinated with. Like Richey, Kurt had been adopted by swathes of youngsters as a tortured spokesperson for an alienated generation.

05

The Samaritans stepped up their advertising campaign in response, using the REM song 'Everybody Hurts' as its theme and music papers printed helpline numbers every week.

In spite of this, there was at least one copycat incident when a 16-year-old Yorkshire girl ran away from home and went missing for three weeks on a pilgrimage around the country in memory of her idol Richey. Thankfully for her family and friends, she returned safe and well.

The band members Richey left behind can still make little sense of his disappearance. "The week before he disappeared he was in the best spirits I'd seen him in since the first breakdown and I thought he was getting better. Sometimes now I think that he was happy because he knew he was going to do something." (Nicky, The Times, May 1996)

In another attempt to explain Richey's problems in the same interview, Nicky said that the scariest thing was that there had been no deeply traumatising event to precipitate his mental demise. He felt that it was because his childhood had been so happy, that he could not cope with life once he left school and reached an age of responsibility. Nicky continued: "That's the most traumatic thing, having to grow up and realising - as he would put it - that everything was shit. Richey used to say, 'you're born unmarked,' then he'd look at himself and go, 'Now I'm scarred.' They do say that 27 is the optimum time for males to commit suicide or break down, usually because of a longing for a disappearing youth."

In late December 1994, LWT featured the vanishing of Richey on their programme 'Missing' and appealed for any information from the public. Eight people called the show, saying variously that he had been seen in a gay pub in Brighton, begging in Liverpool, busking in Cambridge and reading a book in London.

Detective Sergeant Stephen Morey, of the Metropolitan Police Missing Persons Bureau, is in charge of the case, file number 584C, which includes Richey's name, height (5ft8ins), birthdate, birthplace (Blackwood, Gwent) marks, scars, tattoos ('Useless Generation' tattoo on left arm, the '4Real' scar and another tattoo featuring dialogue from the film 'Apocalypse Now') and the date the report was opened - 2/2/95.

Det Sgt Morey said at the end of 1995: "I would say it would be relatively difficult to have remained anonymous for this period of time in this country. Possible, but difficult. For me, personally, he is no longer with us."

After Richey's disappearance, the rest of the band went to ground. Nicky went back to Wales to play golf and tend his garden, Sean headed to Bristol and James became a regular fixture on the London party scene. Each took stock of the situation in their own way and waited for news, hanging on every phonecall. By April, this became too distant a possibility and the band considered their future.

The remaining trio had a meeting with their manager Martin Hall and Richey's parents to discuss whether they should play together again as a band.

Nicky had previously said: "If it ever comes to the point where Richey's not coming back, we wouldn't continue" - but they joined the ranks of bands such as The Charlatans, AC/DC, The Who, The Beach Boys, Metallica, New York Dolls, The Pretenders and Canned Heat by deciding to carry on following the demise of one of their founding members.

Richey's father had expressed the wish that he wanted the band to continue recording and touring as soon as possible as they felt it might "flush him out", which helped resolve the band's minds.

They started to rehearse again that month in Cardiff and continued the work they had started with Richey that January. In the bundle of lyrics he had left them before he disappeared, they had enough to fill three albums.

In August, they publicly announced their intention to continue as a three piece and said they were about to start recording a new album.

It was revealed that what sealed their decision to go ahead had been when Nicky sent James the lyrics to 'A Design for Life'. After James and Sean had written the music, the band all thought they should record an album on the strength of that song alone.

In September, they went to Normandy with producer Mike Hedges, who had previously worked with the likes of McAlmont and Butler. They recorded their first track as a three-piece, their version of Burt Bacharach's 'Raindrops Keep Falling On My Head' for the charity LP 'Help!' to raise money for War Child. While there, they also recorded 'A Design For Life' and later added a string section at London's Abbey Road Studios to achieve a feeling which Nicky described as "a sense of melancholic victory". More tracks were laid down, and during the week that followed, the band travelled to Bath and recorded four new songs, which were later to appear on 'Everything Must Go', using lyrics that Richey had left the band in January. These included 'Elvis Impersonator', 'The Girl Who Wanted To Be God', 'Small Black Flowers That Grow In The Sky' and 'Kevin Carter'. The Manics played their first gig since the disappearance of Richey in December 1995 at London's Wembley Arena supporting The Stone Roses.

UNCERTAIN TIMES

For their very public comeback, the band decided not to perform any songs from 'The Holy Bible' and previewed many of the new songs that would appear on their new album in 1996. Some critics - and possibly some members of the audience - seemed to be concentrating on who was missing rather than the music. The sound was deemed less than adequate, which may have been down to the rumours that the Roses had only allowed the Manics five-minutes to sound-check. However, some saw beyond the fact the Manics were now but three and predicted the band were destined for greater fame than ever that year. As Paul Sexton foresaw at the gig, it certainly was a case of "From despair to here, and then respectfully upwards." (Paul Sexton, The Times, January 1996)

Others were literally moved to tears by the significance of the gig. As Mark Sutherland of NME said: "So tonight is never going to join the list of vintage, incomparable Manic Street Preachers live events. So what? The important thing is: the Manics still exist and what's more, they're playing live and kicking against the pricks." (January, 1996)

MA

"AND IF YOU NEED AN EXPLANATION/THEN EVERYTHING MUST GO/FREED US EVENTUALLY, JUST NEED TO BE HAPPY, HAPPY" (Lyrics from Manic's single 'Everything Must Go' 1996)

CHAPTER 06
A DESIGN FOR LIFE

1996 started off in positive fashion with the Manics. In February, the band announced that they were to release a new single in two months, and in March, just after the Manics had played a gig in Wales as support to Oasis, the announcement that everyone had been waiting for finally came - the Manic Street Preachers were to release their fourth album in May.

They revealed they had recorded 17 new songs and were choosing the final dozen that would appear on their new offering.

The first of these tracks to reach public ears was 'A Design For Life' which they released in April, their first single since 'She Is Suffering' in October 1994. It crashed into the charts at number two and became the band's biggest-selling single to date. Public interest and sympathy were naturally high in the band considering the 15 months since Richey's disappearance, but it was not the reason why the single was so successful. A magic, epic opus, the string-fuelled song was simply one of the most monumental and passionate the Manics had ever released. The beauty of it was only made all the more poignant by the realisation of the band's loss.

But the message was a wider one, of sorrow and anger at the world around them, about the economical and political suppression of the masses. The band had a purpose other than to dwell on the past.

A DESIGN FOR LIFE

Nicky celebrated the song's high debut in the charts with tea at his mother's house. He later telephoned Sherry Edwards, Richey's mum to tell her the news. Sean meanwhile ironed shirts at his home in Bristol. The pair had found contentment in the mundane almost as a panacea to the surreal rock'n'roll life that surrounded them.

Only James marked the occasion in traditional pop star style by sharing drinks with the band's management and friends.

The day after, the band gave their first press interview since Richey's disappearance. Though they remained open-minded about his fate, they also hit out at the strange band of people who insisted the band had knowledge of his whereabouts and swore on their lives that this was not true.

They also revealed that they had set up a trust fund for Richey into which all the royalties for his songs would be paid. It would be open for him for seven years should he ever return. After that time he would legally be declared dead.

"At the end of the day you can't feel grief because you don't know if he's dead. You fell anger, sympathy and sadness. The tragedy lies on a personal level. On a professional level, as a professional band, it doesn't really come into it. You don't think, 'Oh, the band's fucked.' We've known each other too long for that. It's the personal level that's the hardest to take." (Nicky, NME May 4 1996)

Nicky said that he had received treatment for stress-related illness. He was offered Temazepam tranquillisers, but refused.

Despite the success of 'A Design For Life', the legacy of Richey's disappearance was still too painful when the Manics played a secret gig at the Manchester Hacienda in preparation for their support slots at Oasis's Maine Road at the end of April before more than 40,000 people later that month. Nicky came off stage after his performance with rapturous applause rattling in his ears, threw his bass on the floor and promptly burst into tears. The band had not played such a small venue for almost a year and a half and the physical closeness of the audience only seemed to emphasise the space on stage to his left where Richey should have been.

The band's long awaited fourth album 'Everything Must Go' was released on May 20, 1996. Five of the 12 songs on the album feature Richey words, including, poignantly, those of 'Kevin Carter', about the Pulitzer Prize-winning photographer who became famous through a picture he took of a child dying in Rwanda with a vulture standing close by, waiting for the moment of death. Carter later killed himself because he could not live with the resulting celebrity his photograph brought.

Another was 'Removables', which Richey had written three years previously. The band had never managed to write music to the words before, but then someone suggested that they try and capture the spirit of Nirvana's 'Unplugged' album. It proved to be the catalyst the band needed and the track was recorded while the band remembered the day they heard of Nirvana Kurt Cobain's suicide. At the time, they were recording at Britannia Studios, the same place where Joy Division's suicidal lead singer Ian Curtis had made his most bleak, soul-baring records.

The parallels between Curtis and Richey were uncanny. Curtis had hanged himself on the eve of an American tour, May 18 1980. After his death, his lyrics seemed to foretell his fate and some fans of the band thereafter took his black lyrics as a gospel to explain their despair. Some even went as far as to copy Curtis and committed suicide. The band then changed their name to New Order and developed their music away from the claustrophobic melancholia that Curtis had helped shape.

Going back to the Manics, 'Small Black Flowers That Grow In the Sky', another track featuring Richey's lyrics, was written after he had seen a disturbing film about the traumas suffered by animals in town and city zoos. But most lines can be read as a metaphor for Richey's own personal mental prison.

> **"THE PICTURES I CONTEMPLATE PAINTING WOULD CONSTITUTE A HALFWAY STATE AND AN ATTEMPT TO POINT OUT THE DIRECTION OF THE FUTURE - WITHOUT ARRIVING THERE COMPLETELY."** (Jackson Pollock - from the LP sleevenotes of 'Everything Must Go')

06

However, Nicky told Swedish magazine Aftonbladet in May 1996 that they had deliberately attempted to make a more uplifting album than the previous three. "We didn't want to make another manic-depressive album. We couldn't cope with going through the same misery again. But it's still a pretty dark album...it was pretty easy to write, a lot of emotions surfaced and we only needed to catch that."

The Manics, as ever, steadfastly refused to be swayed by the musical fashions of the day, and steered clear of the predominant Britpop sounds that had pervaded much of 1995 and 1996. More to the point, they kept their eyes fixed to the future and refused to attempt to recreate the Manics sound of old. They forged ahead along their own path.

The title track 'Everything Must Go' was a positive message of reconciliation and resolve in the face of adversity and pain. It has become an anthemic definition of the mood of the album. It was also a plea from the band to their fans to accept and understand their decision to continue without Richey - 'Freed from the memory/Escape from our history, history/And I just hope that you can forgive us/But everything must go'.

Nicky said however that the last three tracks on the album 'Interiors', about the troubled artist Willem De Kooning, 'Further Away', the album's love song, and 'No Surface, All Feeling', the tribute to Richey, were his favourites, the more melancholy tracks on the album.

All in all, recording the album had been an easier way for the band to deal with Richey's disappearance than by sitting by the telephone waiting for news of their friend.

'Elvis Impersonator: Blackpool Pier', also by Richey, was about Britain desiring American trash culture and assimilating it into their own.

Although the band had made a concerted effort to try and put the past behind them, it still seems as though the resonance of Richey's absence vibrates through the album from start to finish.

"WE DIDN'T WANT TO MAKE ANOTHER MANIC-DEPRESSIVE ALBUM. WE COULDN'T COPE WITH GOING THROUGH THE SAME MISERY AGAIN. BUT IT'S STILL A PRETTY DARK ALBUM." (Nicky, May 1996)

06

As Nicky said afterwards: "We're really proud of it and I'm sure if Richey ever gets the chance to hear it he'll feel the same".

The band then embarked on a nine-date sell-out UK tour to promote the album. When they played the Wolverhampton Civic Hall just after the album was released, NME's Sylvia Patterson summed up the new Manics mood perfectly, inspired by their "beautiful" rendition that night of 'Motorcycle Emptiness', which made her think of the empty left side of the stage for the first time: "Today, the left isn't even empty any more; it's filled up with everything Richey ever stood for, which was and is The Truth, the man is still with us in his words...the Manics in loss, have gained more than surely even they ever knew they had. On the other side of despair then, behold the invincible." (Sylvia Patterson, NME, May 1996)

The Manics live prowess was further confirmed with electrifying performances at T In The Park on July 14 and at the Phoenix Festival on July 18. Their glorious summer was crowned by the release of the single 'Everything Must Go' which debuted in the charts at number five.

The band had already reached thousands of people with their support gigs for Oasis at Cardiff, Dublin and Manchester for the first half of 1996, and in May they also announced they were to support Oasis at their huge gigs at Loch Lomond and Knebworth Park in August in front of more than 300,000 - a third of a million people - in total.

The Oasis link was further confirmed when the Manics were asked to support the brothers Gallagher and their cohorts on their US tour that September, only the second time they had a chance to show the Yanks what they could do.

06

The overseas jaunt was ill-fated from the start. First of all, Liam refused to go out to the States in favour of going househunting with his fiancee Patsy Kensit and missed the first couple of dates. Then when he eventually relented and flew to meet up with the rest of Oasis, he fought with his brother and Noel stormed back to Britain alone. The tour was cancelled after only three dates. The Manics flew home with the rest of Oasis, but then returned the following weekend to play previously arranged gigs at Seattle, San Francisco, Los Angeles and San Diego.

Despite the opportunity to finally convert America with their musical manifesto, the band still didn't enjoy touring, whether it was the biggest pop music market in the world or not.

In an interview in the States with NME's Keith Cameron, they revealed they would like to become a band like REM, recording lots of albums but not touring for years.

Nicky told him: "Even though I do still enjoy doing gigs when we're on stage, I wouldn't miss it. Especially without Richey. It's the one thing that's incomprehensible." (Nicky, NME, October 996)

Meanwhile, 'Kevin Carter' was released on September 30 and debuted in the UK charts at number nine.

In October, the Manics embarked on yet another sell-out UK tour.

Another single from the album 'Australia', released in December, was Nicky's tale of wanting to flee the aftermath of Richey's disappearance. He wanted to run as far away as possible and as Australia was on the other side of the world, it seemed like the best place to aim for. But

Nicky realised like most people that it doesn't matter how far you run away, you are always left with yourself and your troubles. Instead, he spent three days in Torquay. It has emerged as one of the most uplifting tracks on the album and went straight into the UK charts at number seven. At the end of 1996, the Manics had enjoyed their most successful year to date, concluding the year as one of only three bands to score four top ten UK hits, along with Celine Dion and Boyzone. Nicky summed up the previous 12 months by saying: "Professionally, it's obviously been our most successful year. Sold the most records and the rest of it...A good year on the Richter scale for Manics years. And personally, yeah, it's been alright!" (Nicky, NME Dec 1996)

Besides that, they had a string of incredible live performances behind them, including gigs at T In The Park, Phoenix Festival and the London Royal Albert Hall, so fittingly, they celebrated the end of the year with more gigs, including one at the London Shepherd's Bush Empire, a joyous affair graced with a guest appearance on stage by pop goddess Kylie Minogue, one of the Manics' all-time heroines.

Few people in the audience could help but contemplate the achievement of the band to be there still after five years. The train of thought was hard to avoid with a giant screen behind the band showing films of the four young, innocent and wide panda-eyed wannabe stars at the start of their career. Now, they were just three, toned down, camouflage gear and make up gone. But they had got where they wanted to be. It was a bittersweet victory. They were older, different and undoubtedly wiser. But they were still there.

CHAPTER 07
EVERYTHING GOES ON

Despite the band's resolute focus on the future and their discomfort at dwelling on the past, it's hard not to compare their achievements so far in 1997 with what has gone before. The band temper their delight at success with sad thoughts for their missing friend and band mate.

Whereas in January 1994, Richey had given an interview at the NME Brat Awards speaking of his depression and despondent feelings towards life, in January 1997, the band won three awards at the ceremony, more than any other band at the event, the first time they had achieved such a feat. They had already topped a host of reader's polls in music magazines throughout Britain, but had no trophy to show for a reward. At the Brats, they won Best LP for 'Everything Must Go', Best Single for 'Design For Life' and Best Live Act, all voted for by NME readers. Once Nicky had the first award in his hand, he dedicated it to Richey.

The following month, on February 24, the Manics won two prestigious Brit Awards, for Best Band and Best LP for 'Everything Must Go' - arguably the two most important trophies on offer in what is the biggest annual award ceremony in British Music.

As James picked up the statuette for best group, he said: "I've got to dedicate this award to the wisdom of Mr Philip Hall and the coolness and intelligence of Mr Richey Edwards."

As the band achieved this, their greatest accolade to date, they could not forget the two people who had been intrinsic to moulding the band, who had helped them achieve what they have now done - to turn the tide of popular opinion to their favour.

The Manics dominance of the 1997 Brit Awards was symbolic to anyone who had followed their story. Where they were once sneeringly dismissed by all but the most visionary of critics, they are now acclaimed as one of the greatest bands in British music. All the people sitting at the Manics table at the ceremony found it virtually impossible to fight back tears of joy and sadness as they celebrated the present and acknowledged the past.

This brings us up to date with the story of the band who are now, officially, one of Britain's favourite pop groups. But as they inferred in the title of their 1993 single 'From Despair To Where?' what does the future hold of them? Will they continue as a trio?

After all, wasn't Richey's demise, the band's central, unshakeable despair, the fault of rock'n'roll stardom, the holy grail they had always pursued? James thought not. "I don't think of it as a natural extension of being in a rock group. It might have accelerated it but that's all. In some ways, Richey's a very Richard Briers person, very cardigan, pipe and slippers. But I think if he'd gone on to become a lecturer - which he might well have done - the same thing could have very easily happened, perhaps in a more private way." (James, Q 1994)

Is he still alive? Nicky thinks so. "Deep down, my gut feeling is that he's alive. But that's not based on any logical evidence. I just try to tell myself that he's done what he wanted to. Whatever that is." (The Times, May 1996)

Maybe as Nicky has said, Richey will return to the world a happy man, complete with a long beard and the best book ever written tucked under his arm. Whatever, he knows, as do the rest of the band and each and every Manics fan, that it's difficult to accept that anyone is dead without a body.

Until then there is always hope. But if he is alive, it's obvious that he doesn't want to be found. Regardless of the undisclosed truth of the matter, there is still no full stop to the mystery of Richey's disappearance, so the band are resigned to remain philosophical and take events on a day to day basis.

"When there's nature, or where there is breathing, there are true moments of joy. You've just got to recognise them. And not take them for granted. And that's what I try to do, have moments of elation in life, however small, five minutes a day, and be able to think 'Yeah, that'll do. That'll do me now.'" (Nicky, Vox October 1996)

In fact, Nicky has admitted he's grateful that he's still here and not in an institution somewhere. No other band has gone through what the Manics have throughout their history. And so we're glad that the Manics and their music are still here too and we hope and pray they will continue to release some of the most passionate, uplifting, thought-provoking and magical rock music this country has ever produced.

Perhaps the French philosopher Jean-Paul Sartre was right. "La fie commence a l'autre cots du desepoir." Or in English, life begins on the other side of despair.

07

PERHAPS THE FRENCH PHILOSOPHER JEAN-PAUL SARTRE WAS RIGHT. "LA FIE COMMENCE A L'AUTRE COTS DU DESEPOIR." OR IN ENGLISH, LIFE BEGINS ON THE OTHER SIDE OF DESPAIR.